This is Lt James
own copy which
he sent me
from Susan.

The marks of
pasteins are his

[signature]
May 29/12

Note Found in the Desert

David! you've been the best friend a man in my position could have

St. James

The Fifty Lost Poems of

Saint James Harris Wood

The Moon Again, What Are My Eyes Like? (she asked), and A List of Unknown Reasons first appeared in *Takahe*

My Dark Irish Dream, *Grasslimb*

Breathing in the Universe, *Chapman*

Trapped in her Mouth, Throwing a Quiet Fit (Waiting to be noticed), My System of Record Keeping (less than state of the art), The Nightclub Singer (In the Mad Part of Town), Lines of Barbed Wire, Double Damned (inner dialogue after arrest in a night club), The Last Step, *The SHOp*

The Illusion of Understanding (1 Mathematician in 2 Bodies), *LiNQ*

One Single Breath, *The Sun*

The Restraining (Disorder), *On Spec*

Narcotic Theory (of Sexual Relativity), *Confrontation*

Wake Down, *Planet*

The Lost Subway Home, *Van Gogh's Ear*

Not Hell (...but), *Tears in the Fence*

Physics be Damned, *Dreams and Nightmares*

Note Found in the Desert, *Space and Time*

Torturing the Young Primitives, *Stinging Fly*

My Prison, *Rosebud*

AUTHOR'S NOTE

I wrote most of these poems while living in a desert penal colony at the edge of the Mojave. I am not a bad man, but a careless one. I never hurt one single person in my life except my family and friends and most especially my sons, whom I abandoned by screwing up and landing in prison. I played music with drug addicts and maniacs from whom I picked up a heroin smoking habit which led to a bankrobbing habit (no guns, only innuendo). I've been very lucky as my sons (Lowell, Dylan, and Zachary) and family have continued to love and support me during my stay in the crucible. and fortunate to have found new friends: Robert Bixby, of March Street Press, *The Sun*'s Sy Safransky, John and Hilary Wakeman from *The SHOp* in Ireland, David Caddy from *Tears in the Fence* in England, Valerie Polichar, from *Grasslimbs,* and Diane Walton from *On Spec* in Canada, and many others who've published my work and given me invaluable advice. One of my friends here in the hellhole, David Berlin, created the cover art. Both of us love to get mail and will reply to anyone who cares to write.

The Poet
Saint James Harris Wood T30027
PO Box 8101/CMC-6223
San Luis Obispo, CA 93409

The Artist
David Berlin T01637
PO Box 8101
San Luis Obispo, CA 93409

Note
Found
in the
Desert

THE MOON AGAIN

Can I hold the moon again,
carefully with both hands
above my head towards the stars.
Never let it go, I know
it pulls the rain away
from my face and holds the sun
in its arms while the world sleeps.
I reach all the way round
the craters made with fallen stars,
mountains of late night prayers,
my face warm with the history
of the dusty lunatic orb
that I took for granted and lost.

Through my small window
watching the night rise from the ground
to the moon, wanting in the dark.
Can I flee—a ghost released, a meteor –
from this broken clock, my flesh.
Has the world forgotten the tides
washing the hole where the moon once lived,
scraping the splinters of my broken bones;
will there be one last communion,
salt on my breath, lips draped and trembling,
the moon light red with unanswered prayer.

MY DARK
IRISH DREAM

Wears her nightgown to Saint Pat's parade,
it is black, she is beautiful,
standing up for lunacy, unafraid.
Irishmen dance, jigs and hip hop.

Her eyes are as red as her heart,
thick with midnight blood,
fixed on imaginary stars,
full of history and lies.

Beer flows like an angry river,
to her knees, to her hips;
she swims from bar to bar,
singing at the top of her lungs.

She gets so mad—she starts to cry,
slowly crumbling to pieces;
steals a hat from a drunken pianist,
and paddles home to bed.

BREATHING
IN THE UNIVERSE

Sighs escape
the sound, the air, the act
drawn from some
light years distant
soft raspy exhalations
allowing distant elements
singular, unbound
to fill the void
surrounding her
composing what's real
differently
which no machine
can imagine
every tattered idea
turned outside in
as her mouth,
opens wider to exhale
pieces of stars
distance unrecognized
every sigh a memory
of all the space
asking to be filled
within her
another sigh the only sign
she is breathing
in the universe.

REHABILITATION BY ORDEAL

Darkness, like gasoline
Concrete
hard and mean
Electricity, runs wild
broken
fences
mile after mile
Eagles walk
in the desert
Hitchhikers
sell tambourines
Darkness, with soup and bread
Barbed wire
running out of breath

TRAPPED
IN HER MOUTH

Strange goddess or starving peasant,
she takes me,
clutching my hip,
an eye rolled up, her gaze
pinning me to the mattress
demanding that I die
one last time
with the grace of a begging man
trapped in her mouth
like a moth.
And after she's dealt with
my lamentable needs,
displays her millionaire's teeth,
tosses a toaster
in the tub
to restart my heart
as I lay there
exhausted, watching her,
big hipped and flat footed
walking erotically away
like a woman who's had
a good time,
had a few children
and has a good idea
about what she wants.

THE ILLUSION OF UNDERSTANDING

(1 Mathematician in 2 Bodies)

The brothers Chudovsky
claim to be one
mathematician/
and in their spare time
they calculate pi/
which is an endless
number with no
discernable pattern/
something that drives
math men mad...

Although they were nearly
unemployed
completely untenured
panhandling grants
and consulting fees/
they decided to build
a supercomputer
fashioned from parts
received in the mail
probably from companies
nearly on the verge
of bankruptcy themselves
if their client base
is composed

of people seeking
to define the infinite/

So, the Chudovskys
in their own home
built this machine
that became overwrought/
overheating needing
industrial air conditioners
and 26 fans while seeking
mythical numbers/

Though confounded,
the beleaguered machine
calculated pi to
two billion one million
nine hundred and seven
decimal places/ and yet
the end is not in sight/

While many poets aren't sure
what the ratio of the
circumference of a circle
to its diameter means
or why its important/
one notices that
poems finally end//

ONE SINGLE BREATH

I take a breath,
it's mine,
I need it. Then the world
takes it back.
I don't know
how to feel
about the loss,
so I hold
the next breath
and wait,
knowing the world
would have me die
rather than relinquish
one mouthful of its air,
and I wonder,
should I die,
could I somehow
keep the mouthful
of air,
thereby finally
winning
some small
prize,
besides the obvious
one
of my escape.

THE RESTRAINING
(Disorder)

He trained three homing pigeons
to fly back in time
towards the nest
where they'd been born
carrying messages
made of magnetism
tips on the stock market
to his long dead wife.

He wanted time to know
that he still loved her
cared about her finances
and eventual reincarnation.

The first pigeon got lost
captured by a shaman
baked into a pie
used to seduce a warrior.

The second went sideways
into an alternate take
where pigeons were seen as signs
stuffed, bronzed and contemplated.

The third went forward
a thousand years or so
found the wife who wept
at the memory
of her former life
and the man
who wouldn't let go.

WHY I LEFT

(speech made, standing on a coffee table)

Oh...
I have a list,
a glorious manifestation
of the barbarisms you practice.
Yes,
I'd tell you,
but unfortunately for everyone,
I'd rather the suffering go on, undefined.
Every,
nerve in my mouth
stands on end, fitfully begging,
to lash, to vent...this thing.
To be...
the bigger person,
a giant! I keep my own counsel
and let you alone, bathe in pettiness.
What!
in the world
did I do to anger
the goddesses of passive aggression?
I'm crazy?
Ha! There's your proof:
my madness directly correlates
to whatever the hell is wrong with you.
Love (?),
I don't know,
I remember...I don't know;

a beautiful whore with diamonds in her.
No,
don't look at me;
your eyes set skin on fire;
that no whiskey will ever quench.
Don't cry,
it sickens me;
the tears are only lubricant
for the next episode's excesses.
Thanks!
now I'm abstract,
your loves tastes like electricity,
the diamonds sold to lesbian lawyers.
Don't,
try to talk;
I believe what I believe I believe,
mouths are for butterscotch and car crashes.
So...
          are we straight?

NARCOTIC THEORY

(of Sexual Relativity)

I remember one particular night,
in a hotel room,
we'd been on the run
for months on end,
or maybe a year or two,
it's hard to say,
time had become
one of those affairs
Einstein dreamt about,
a relative to unsure things,
not always now necessarily,
but never passing
in that hotel room,
our narcotic stained blood
held you in my arms,
unaccountable, sweaty,
straining at the inevitable
sound of police cars,
passing in the night;
you cried my name,
begging to be,
pinned to the sheets by a thousand crimes
documented by whispers,
who love to see you
harnessed like a mad woman
in our crooked bed;
with blackmailers for neighbors,

broken hands and lights
in the window,
sweat so sweet
lubricating
that dark road;
until dawn
threw bricks of light
shattering, exposing, igniting
the beauty of your flesh
in a hotel room, a hundred years or so, ago.

WAKE DOWN

Night dissolves into day,
while mocking birds cry
of alarm clocks and cell phones.
Dogs in a 100 yards, awake
from dreams of paper boys
living in the wild.
A distant bus grinds coffee,
while eggs and bacon
glumly crawl
into frying pans.
Racoons and possums
pick up their feet,
and nod to the cats
on the next shift.
The moon, a high diver,
falls into the sea
waking up the sun.
Early risers study the sky
like generals losing a war;
marching orders are issued
to groggy clouds
and commuters shuffling
into the underground.
Traffic jams and elevators
fall and rise, rise and fall.
Shadows born
start towards noon,
onward to the horizon,
until day
seeps into night.

THE LOST
SUBWAY HOME

A thousand dollar guitar stuck in her back,
a purse made of chocolate and morphine,
hair black, white and red, and to her waist;
a practical promiscuity, tempered during
an unknown number of drunken late night
assignations with Russian poets
who run away in every city.

In a bar abandoned by the literate—
leaving only surly foreign revolutionaries
masquerading as drug dealers; and elderly
punk rock anarchists who sold out to
the man and rockabilly—she demanded
frankly that I go with her like she was
god, a cop and a prostitute all mixed up in
one ripe perspiring ball of feminine fuck.

Rode together all night for miles
on the city subway that had been lost
for thirteen days, full of late night
maniacs; depressed middle aged burglars;
a couple of wandering folk singers
who specialized in rants attacking the
Department of Motor Vehicles; and two
escaped Venezuelan monkeys.

The house—three shadowy black velvet
draped bedrooms filled with neurotic
sculptures, drug paraphernalia and
magazines promoting Japanese fetish
cults, shared with four unemployed
cocktail waitresses—smelled
interesting as if a rock festival had
recently done its thing in the living room.

Fortune left us alone for an hour,
all the strangeness fell away,
leaving a woman that only required
that I conquer the void,
tap what's hidden, which we did,
and I momentarily felt a way
I wish I could forever.

A long lonely ride back in the lost subway car,
now empty except for an unconscious grifter,
and two mimes trapped inside a noisy world;
I wonder why I'm not stranger, strange
as the fragrant home of the woman
with a guitar stuck in her back,
strange as the warm aroma
that clings to me even now.

THROWING
A QUIET FIT
(Waiting to be noticed)

Standing still
in the backyard
radiating
a low brood
among the bees
busy with survival
who have no time
for complicated
romance.
Grass grows
beneath my shoes
struggling
with the weight,
unaware of the
bigger issues.
The sun slips
slowly
towards the roof
marking another
day of the woman's
ability to ignore
agonized daydreaming.
The garden continues
brutally on,
roses rising and

falling to pieces,
troops of acrobatic
spiders weaving traps
careless and ignorant
of the leisure time
we lofty, cloud kissing
creatures have to waste
on mating ritual.
A black beetle
spends half his life
waddling to death
in order to
witlessly fulfill
his mate's
only demand,
while I wonder
if she's even noticed
my silent brood.
A neighbor cat
scrambles up the fence,
scoffs at my tactic,
then leaps
to destroy
an outpost of potato bugs
at the foot of
a willow that's been brooding since
the turn of the century.
I study the sky
and the upstairs
window

from the corner
of my eye
hoping my foolish
vigil has done more
than mark the ecology
of this suburban
day.

MY SYSTEM
OF RECORD KEEPING
(less than state of the art)

There are piles of paper, everywhere,
some in Latin, some on fire,
boxes of documents and carbon copies
of unpaid foreign traffic tickets;
by bad fate a former roommate
left behind an entire city of real estate—
deeds, transaction reports, forged titles
and pictures of a homeless women's shelter.
My missing social security card
generated a nationally ranked archive
of correspondence from the government,
an account of their malfeasance
more complicated than the charter
of an impoverished third world nation.
Warranties and receipts testifying
to the existence of a now dead vacuum
are mixed up with love letters
from a South American woman
who broke it off after I inadvertently
sent her a pornographic postcard
intended for an old college buddy
currently residing in an extravagant
federal prison near Stockton
for counterfeiting and naturally
he left his entire supply

of ill-gotten currency paper
and telephone books from all over
in my already beleagured attic.

So, pressed to prove that I exist,
with high school pictures
and birth certificates,
I sigh and tip over a filing cabinet,
wondering if the paper world
contains even a shred
of me.

THE SKY IS MINE

Thought I saw a falling star,
landed in the backyard,
fell so slowly,
falling like it knows me.
Put on my mocking coat
and a pair of old jeans,
couldn't find a flashlight,
went on out the back door.
Shallow stars were shining
on a broken wine glass,
a lost bird snoring,
stuck up in a willow tree.
Barefoot in the dewy grass,
might of crushed a caterpillar,
crawl up on a picnic table,
forgot what I'm looking for.
Stare up into the darkness
of the endless universe,
wonder what I want,
wonder's all I have.
Thought I saw a falling star,
landed in the backyard,
pick it up slowly,
everybody knows me.

THE TROUBLESOME BOOK REPORT

This was going to be my best book report;
lengthy (unlike my usual, which is often short),
with footnotes and insights and grand digressions;
unfortunately, instead, I've a sad confession,
or, maybe, more like a sound explanation.
Imagine if you can, my total frustration
at having the best, world class intentions,
then I become, a candidate for detention.

I went to the book store, as the teacher proposed,
perhaps a little late, it was inexplicably closed.
Okay, it was nineish, they'd been closed for hours;
but I had done nearly everything in my power:
missed a bus, chased a dog, got caught in the rain,
lost a hat, saw a friend, played a few video games;
and time has a way of passing, just like a shot.
Bottom line, I was supposed to get a book, I did not.

A couple days passed, the matter slipped my mind,
it's happened before, it's how I'm designed.
Did I mention it was Dickens, who engineered my fall,
and Oliver Twist, the orphan, at the root of it all?
Now, it was one of those books, made into a movie;
so, I rented the video like thousands before me.
Right at the beginning, I knew something was wrong,

when Oliver immediately, burst into song.

Obviously I'm no expert, but this was unusual.
Charles Dickens, never wrote a musical.
All my hopes as a book reporter died,
even though I so plainly tried.
I beg that you accept this poem as a report.
It is grand, you must admit, though a little short.
Give me a day or two to work a song into the text,
I absolutely guarantee, it will be the best.

TO BE GONE

I stand in the wind
sniffing the air
wishing it would take me
to the places I smell
pulling my feet
up off the ground
mussing my hair
rearranging my clothes
changing me
I'd gladly give myself
to the sky
eyes closed
floating to anywhere
except the ground
beneath my feet
the dirt so familiar
the same horizon
dogging my days
how I long
to be gone.

A LIST OF UNKNOWN REASONS

She left me
in the middle of the night.
Golden silver stars
heroically fading,
streetlights marching
towards the horizon,
hound dogs muttering
midnight theories,
and owls howling
in the key of C
on an upper branch
hidden
by a flock
of crows who ordinarily
left owls to the vagaries
of
bored old farmers
with shotguns and little boys
who typically have
a deadly rock tucked away.

She took the truck
loaded earlier in the day,
with every chair I owned
(I noticed their absence
at dinner but didn't want
to be defeated in another
conversation about
selfishness), 15 pairs of
my blue jeans destined to
be sold to immigrants who
believe the jeans give
magic powers, and a
nearly dead harmonica
I used to harass dogs.
She left me
her phone book and acoustic
piano which still plays
dark songs
written by arguments.
Left her clothes stacked
in the kitchen,
a pair of worn panties,
smell of aloe and sex,
wrapped around the heart
I lost and a list of

reasons
reasons so
far afield
of what I thought
had happened,
that I could spend
the rest of my life
turning each one
into a musical.

SHE BELIEVED ME MAD

(I was never lonelier)

I loved her, in my way,
for two long years
because she was beautiful
and listened to me,
catered to my eccentricities,
accepted my compliments with grace,
made love out of idle hours,
sweet instinct and ordinary need.

I would talk for hours,
from Timothy Leary to String Theory,
warm in the glow of her patience,
content to be venting
in the safety of our home,
though I wondered when
and where she believed.

The day arrived, she concluded
that there is more to life
than religious promiscuity
and non-stop urban adventure.
After she packed her things
she took my hand and sadly whispered
"I never understood
a word you said."

THE MOON,
THE STARS,
THE SUN
(in be minor)

The moon is crooning lullabies
comparing sleep to death
casting shadows on the sea
clouds on its breath.

Stars are falling in love
with their own wishes
crashing into mansions
breaking all the dishes.

The sun is hiding out
other side of the world
bedraggled and bewildered
a burnt and tarnished pearl.

THE CHIHUAHUA WHO
RUINED MY LOVE LIFE

She had a Chihuahua,
ferocious and absurd, who would snarl at me,
his face full of loss and dementia.

He may have loved her,
and so bent his entire life
towards foiling my romantic ambitions.

I tried to be friendly
with snacks and caresses; only rewarded
with unchecked Latin rage and contempt.

It became apparent
that the Chihuahua would never come around;
something inside me broke, went dark.

Not myself,
I turned obsessive, wanting retribution
against the tiny terrorist, measure for measure.

The day came,
caught him unaware, asleep like a fool;
put a sock on his head, spun him on the kitchen floor.

The Chihuahua found his feet,

growled barbarically and ran into the wall,
went instantly mad, attacking sound and shadow.

Realizing that perhaps
I'd gone too far, I plucked the sock off his head,
leapt nimbly to safety, onto the kitchen table.

The Chihuahua ran in circles
and screamed; shaking and scrabbling,
charged out of the room, under a bed in the back.

So, matters weren't improved,
were actually worse; if I entered the house
the foul creature would foam and simulate a stroke.

I decided I needed
a dog ten times as big, to put the little killer
in his rightful place, teach him consequence.

I acquired a Weimaraner,
a monster I supposed, with a mouth big enough
to swallow in a gulp, the hairless Mexican dog.

I always think
things simple and finite, never taking into account
the unpredictability of every variable.

I arrived at the house

with the alleged monster, who unpredictably wanted
to play with the puny evil dog, who had the usual in mind.

The Chihuahua flew through the air
like an indignant pirhana, latched onto the snout
of the discredited Weimaraner, now hurt and disenchanted.

The big dog shook the little,
who hung on with every intention of staying forever,
belligerent and insane, to prove the world wrong.

The Weimaraner ran,
daft with pain, out the door, down the street,
for hundreds or miles, as far as I know.

For the Chihuahua and the Weimaraner
were never seen again; rumors from the hinterlands
claim strange sights, late at night, in childrens' dreams.

This episode
did not endear me to the Chihuahua's mistress;
I moved on to a woman, with a lunatic Siamese.

THE
NIGHTCLUB
SINGER
(In The Mad Part of Town)

He screamed
like one of those
old mad Rhythm and Blues
singers, Picket and Wolf
come to mind; except that
where the old school cats
cried out
with a certain drunken joy,
his wail carried abject
and undisguised
reckless threat
tempered by desolation,
without benefit of clergy
or pharmaceuticals;
raising the dead,
lowering his blood pressure,
climbing a mountain,
scaring away the crows,
knocking over drinks,
and breaking all the clocks.

The band plays on,
tethered to the stage

by an African back beat
and rock hard dissonance,
ignoring the screams
but carrying his body
down the river,
into the sea.

LINES OF
BARBED WIRE

The prison poets gather
in the multi-purpose room
recently abandoned
by a troop of yogis
and soon to be occupied
by a discussion group
of critical thinkers
tired of society.

The poets have nothing...
in the world,
in common,
in their hands,
and hope that gathering
will help them find
some small shred
of communication.

The guard locks the door
and bangs on the window,
letting the poets know
that their fraternity
of rhymers and rune
are nothing more
than numbers
and an inconvenience.

The poets pull
their chains and chairs
into a circle
all their own,
facing each other,
rustling papers and the horses
in their heads...
they write off
into the hills.

DOUBLE DAMNED

(inner dialogue after arrest in a night club)

 And I leave the scene,
like a Shakespearean character,
whose life is hell,
hauled away by the soldiers
and beaten offstage;
infected by a mad European slut,
her family enjoys, killing her lovers.
Villagers are dancing,
to this godforsaken music,
they all have knives
and psychiatric conditions;
even the curtain collapses,
breaking the crippled boy's neck,
his dog morosely grieving,
bites any number of extras.
Then his Majesty the King,
demands satisfaction,
frightening characters,
high and low,
to engineer a distraction.
Whereupon...
everyone bursts into song,
about a prince gently killed
by his wife's other husband,
and it goes on and on,
'til patience is spent,

ending the episode,
with I, as ignorant as ever,
alone in a cell on a telephone,
calling the cast, trying to make bail.

BLACKOUT ON MELROSE
(Rosa's burglar suite)

Cold and broken
roaming the wilds of the fashionable district,
it was late
in the day and the depths of our need.
Melrose and Vine,
so Hollywood it wore makeup and hurt;
taxi cabs
swollen with tourists and imported gigolos
coasted along
with nowhere to go, they always arrive.
In the hills above
laying in wait like Spanish conquistadors:
poets, thieves,
scofflaws on cocaine, double dealing 1 armed men,
sullen blackmailers,
And 17 year old girls with daddy's pistol;
and though the moon
seemed to shine, to those in the know
it was fading,
exactly the same as sweet Rosa and I
as we skulked
along Melrose with only hours to live
the way we liked;
studying, everything that moved or shined,
all the signs—
disoriented narcotic wolves, always watching
waiting,
delighted and afraid of the unknown variable.

Dancers exploded
onto the street from the last late night bar,
eyeing the feral aura
shamelessly reaching for their valuables.
Rosa smiles,
making the mark doubt his own sense;
no matter,
we don't desire confrontation, only property,
the negotiable:
unlocked cars, castles, wayward wallets, pianos,
trust or faith.
Even Judas closed his eyes during the last kiss,
unwilling to know
the expression, the flinch, the broken heart.
Witnesses are required
to document miracles and convict criminals;
so we wait,
until the last pedestrian marches listlessly
to home and hearth,
leaving the city seduced and compliant
all for us.
As it grew late, Rosa and I, shifty eyed,
felt the little trap.
Periodically a car floated carefully by
under the streetlights,
and though every store and haberdashery
lay lifeless,
something would as something always did,
happen;
for our god is an indulgent and divine thief
who sympathizes...

...and so, a power grid nervously broke down,
every lamp died,
bringing us home, unseen, uncatchable,
full of dark promise.
We laughed like naked drunken millionaires
duping the poor,
went into well practiced action, our senses
in love with midnight
trapped in between the days, every moment dark,
filled with sighs,
contraband, illegal blood and wily cats.
We crept up and down
the blacked out street whispering strategies.
The god of thieves
drew my eye to an ancient air conditioner;
one small push,
it fell into a vintage leather and cotton store,
full of swag.
After the crash, a serene and pure moment;
no one within miles,
the entire district deserted for our pleasure.
Mad as hatters
being fucked with their hair on fire,
we slithered,
carelessly, joyously, seeing months of solvency,
the hapless store
ours for the taking, for the evening.

Rosa shyly modeled
an honest to god floor length coat
made from the fur
of completely naked and long dead African monkeys.
We made two piles,
foreign and domestic, of leather jackets
destined to be sold
to local motorcycle gangs and pawn shops.
Arms full,
wearing her dead jungle coat, Rosa scampered
back out the window
to retrieve our partner in life and crime,
a broken down Ford,
unloved by others, dented, addled, low blue book,
cherished by us,
yet destined months later to be traded
for a gram of dope;
however, on that night, brother car exploded
with finery:
Shakespearean cloaks, Parisian military jackets,
Hawaiian shirts
sporting bloody flamingos once worn by Filipinos,
and every damn thing
all self-respecting vainglorious thieves dream about,
worth thousands,
which in our drug saturated world is millions...
millions I tell you.

I shoved our wild god given spoils
out the hole,
setting them free into the streets of commerce.
Rosa she ran
back and forth from the swag to the Ford
parked down the block;
she is so beautiful that I want to take her
there on the spot,
which goes to show how easily distracted,
studiously reckless
I am bound to be, a nationally ranked fool.
While my eye
was off the ball, dreaming of dispensations
and carnal indulgence,
a team of opportunistic homosexual streetwalkers
boldly stole off
with a half dozen World War II leather jackets
with fake fur collars,
suddenly more precious than anything else
now that they were lost.
Rosa she danced and screamed in a furious temper,
causing me to stop
and see the streets we imagined abandoned,
crawling with whores,
each and all ready to change their careers
from hookers
to intrepid burglars guided by our same wild god,
I imagine,
to covet, liberate and liquidate stray valuables,

starting with our hoard.
Cold and brave, Rosa made an executive decision
to retreat to the car
filled to the brim with rarities and collectibles,
ironic treasures
possibly once worn by senators and circus folk,
none like us,
not on the run, nor insane, or else the clothes
would have been destroyed
by angry spouses, homicide detectives and psychiatrists.
I put on a beret
designed by the King of Arizona in 1927,
cocky and sure,
(the beret, not the king, he loathed himself).
"Homeward darling,"
I advised my coconspirator, driver and mad lover...

...the car, wouldn't start.

A lonely trumpet blew, flags flew at half mast
all across town,
half crocked birds fell from the sky,
half the criminals
in the city lockup felt the familiar chill
of catastrophe.
Rosa raised her eyebrow to say what the fuck,
whatever and Jesus Christ.
We sat in the dead car dark, mulling mad chance,
bad fate and circumstance,
though every thing that ever went wrong

was like we planned it,
our divine force, an inconsistent advocate.
A security guard
pulled up behind us, cutting the blackout
with a spotlight.
In a crouch the local law circled our car,
a Greek wrestler
looking to be the casual death of us both.
But Rosa is sly,
she sashays from the irresponsible Ford,
hand on her hip,
looking lost rather than a cat burglar,
locks eyes with the guard.
"Oh courageous and noble supplier of security,
we're simple merchants
whose car, like the city, has given up the ghost."

Security's name is bob.
He had a hat, a car with a radio, little else.
Moving from Ohio,
he wanted to act, against the advice of everyone
in his world—
failed spectacularly, not a single part,
even as an extra.
Lovely Rosa was the first woman in 7 years
with a kind word.
Poor old bob said, "My humble cables beg
to jump your car."
Graciously we consented, and while he reasoned
with our engine,

Rosa stole his flashlight, hat and girlie magazine
out of sheer whimsy.
"Give her a try!" bob shouted, all in white,
glad to be of aid
in the dark and troubled city during a crisis
that reminded him
of a movie he'd auditioned for back in the day
when hope could breathe.
The car started up bashfully, like a felon
who'd taken a nap
on the job just to keep things interesting.

Rosa drove us off
into the fading moon, wondering how
we stay alive,
what with the high cost of the unknown,
though we're in love,
at least with ourselves and maybe each other;
the ruins of Los Angeles
cuddles our guile and forthright inclinations,
making the night
and breaking the hearts of every mother's dream
that comes to Hollywood.

IT WAS MIDNIGHT

...on the east side.
I know now not to trust any night
that features a moon that eats itself.
Harmonicas honked, drunks were
barking.

Staring at her soft white shoulders
in that warm spring dress,
blue true eyes in the dim bar light;
tired negroes danced,
sad musicians played
the sound of a distant train crash.

Her words were little saints
flown in from distant climes,
snatching the last remnants
of my reservations.
Agile as always I surrendered,
disobeying long standing policy,
that words were worthless.

one a.m....
blood on my shirt,
hid the last shreds of myself
in her purse,
bid them farewell

with contempt,
willing
to put an eye out
with a martini swizzle stick
to prove something or another.

two a.m.
the dance is exhausted,
waitresses threaten and flirt,
final rites performed
with southern whiskey.
Kissed my fingers
for they'd soon be inside.
Slid into the parking lot
where her curious tribes' people –
rakes, fops, sots and gamblers –
stared at me.

"If any pain is to be borne,
it will be by me."
I always say that;
I'm always lying.
Lightning smashed the sky.

three thirty a.m. ...
we escaped in her foreign van
onto a suburban side street.

Events were insistent and convincing;
cats watched and discussed our habits
(like two hands
clasped and praying),
the birds in the trees
discussed the cats,
all agreed how easily,
with one soft word,
civilization is shed.

later on...
we laughed, she cried,
went to a movie,
ate a chicken pot pie.
Her dog was dismayed,
then grudgingly tolerant,
finally secretly delighted
when I used him to soak up water
ritualistically spilled
throughout the apartment
in a failed bid to mark territory.

then...
well, I don't know,
words make little sense,
they mill around
like crippled idiots.

I wish the stupid fuckers
would leave me alone
like she did.

months later...
it was midnight in the north county.
I sit brooding;
yuppies compliment my music,
it seems like a personal attack;
management asks me to adjust the volume.
I'd rather be banned for life.

NOT HELL
(but...)

And though this isn't hell, it's in the suburbs
Where the houses aren't on fire, but smell of mold;
The buses don't explode in death, but are late and lost;
You aren't burnt forever, but bored unto death.

And though this isn't hell, it's maybe a cousin
Who doesn't torture animals, but dresses them up;
Whose woman isn't half mad/half creature,
But hates you and eats cigarettes.

This isn't hell, but it knows of it,
About the subtle road to your heart.
No one is likely to buy your soul;
There is no interest whatsoever.

TWO SAD GIRLS
(TechnologicalLonging)

Wearing only a tattered
dirty pink T-shirt
with a torn red sock
tied around her waist,
she has no shoes or bed,
food only every other day,
never set foot in a car,
airplanes are only machines
that fly through her dreams,
family is nothing,
a rumor, a lie.

At fourteen she wanders
through the city's alleys,
hiding in the shadows
of avant-garde skyscrapers
miles above the rabble,
made of neoteric synthetics,
designed to cow, crowded
with drunken millionaires
who will never see
her shrunken stomach
and weary brown eyes.

In the depths of the darkest alley,
looking for edible garbage,
she comes upon a cell phone,
alive, fully charged,
the priceless deluxe model,
a diamond glistening,
tool of her oppressors,
mysterious like ancient Egyptians,
capable of contacting the moon
and every wealthy man
who ever lived.

Random chance
(being her life)
pushed a button summoning
an angry heir to a fortune
that demanded he swear
at anyone who couldn't
be bought or compromised;
like a ghoul he needed
the blood of corporation,
the fealty of executives;
he quickly ascertained she only
deserved a curse and a disconnect.

Chance next called another
girl of fourteen in a boarding school,
also lost except
her world was catered,
insured, carpeted and warm.
"Daddy?" she asked softly, hopelessly.
The street girl sighed
into the phone, an expression
of abandonment,
more basic than the rich girl's,
yet they recognized each other
and sighed for hours—
til the phone died.

PHYSICS
BE DAMNED

Falling stars are fleeing,
wishing on themselves
to no longer be
part of the dark unknown;
adoring gravity
and the real estate
of a planetary hearth;
sailing light years
through magnetic radiation,
guided by the steady hand
of perfect mad confidence,
impenetrable physics
and a longing
known by
every shred of matter
that ever left home.

THE LAST STEP

Through that dark door
the night moved
politely among us
weighing souls
counting intentions
knowing each man
like a lost brother
instilling his heart
with bad courage
and the ability
to always find
the devil's party;
every spirit
diminished
by the broken light
the casual void
brutality's
careless grace;
each decision made
with lost innocence.

WHAT ARE MY EYES LIKE?

(she asked)

Like diamonds or fireworks maybe;
a gypsy dog with a stolen chicken;
a motorcycle on its way to Memphis;
every color but one,
staring sightlessly.

Like gasoline aflame
floating down a river
around the bend
lighting the banks on fire,
selling the locals promises.

Like a love song gone bad,
that laughs at unemployed cripples
and harbors disoriented fugitives;
filing away each and every vision
for future prosecution and tax purposes.

They have a franchise
on history and complicated suffering,
a surly cast of thousands
waiting to attack the sun,
then on to an early lunch.

NOTE FOUND
IN THE DESERT
(in the trunk of a burned out car)

I am bleeding, I am fleeing,
careening across the desert.
I am coughing, caught in a dream,
a witless insomniac.
Out in the open, I am hidden
staving off the end.
Mistakes were made, I am sorry
there's no turning back.

I am broken, I am choking,
flailing at the sky.
Hopelessly stalled, I am falling,
a hapless infidel.
Listless, I've been dismissed,
cast into the lowlands.
I am breathing, slow and easy,
at night at last alone.

I am dirty, cold and thirsty,
on a road lost and long.
No moon for days, stars begin to fade,
the signs all disagree.
I see coyotes, walking slowly,
tell my wife I'm fine.
The only witness, I am listening,
like I never did before.

TORTURING
THE YOUNG PRIMITIVES

When my son Zak was six or so,
he'd invite to spend the night
a couple of cousins and a friend or two.
They'd behave tolerably well, watching movies
banned by their mothers until midnight,
inhaling soda pop, eating chocolate in pound lots,
dining on ice cream sundaes and sugary foods
that in retrospect, as a parent, I regret.
When their blood sugar reached a certain stage,
they'd engage in roughhouse, fight and skirmish,
browbeat and brawl reaching for a bombastic bluster—
at which point modern tradition led my son
to formally ask, as if for sacrament,
"Father, torture us! Torture us, I beg you!"
The other children, familiar with our practice,
would cry, "Torture! Torture! Please torture us!"
The torture they refer to is that I chase them
around the house, a broiling free-for-all
in an enormous circle made by the kitchen,
living room and TV den; I take out after them.
The children run like lunatics on fire
bouncing through the house,
skidding around corners,
jumping over and onto couches and chairs,
gleefully yelping, scrabbling, falling
but never stopping they'd roll and scramble

back to their feet, hurl pillows and cushions
in my path, nearly hysterical to escape
an ancient life threatening ritual.
Some split off from the pack to hide,
every child for himself in a riotous rhubarb
until I track them down.
The torture, a mixture of Indian wrist burns,
industrial tickling, gouged collarbones
and other forms of juvenile tribulation
was at worst…nothing really,
except a chance to fall to pieces,
taunted by the swifter crowd
who surround the captured child,
to swagger and dance their guts out
celebrating the failure of the fallen.
The relentless harassing nature of the chase
brought delirious tears of joy to the young primitives;
but the torture, while admired
and cherished for its hands on inspiration—
seemed somehow lacking to me.
Though the children demonstrated real fear,
often nearly breaking into tears
at being so persistently bird-dogged,
I thought the chase could be better served
as an ordeal
if the consequences were more traumatic.
No lasting injury could be tolerated of course;
the mothers already saw me
as a renegade who needed curtailing.
Bitter moms still held memories of skinned elbows

and a bloody lip collected
during a midnight dark basketball game. So...
on this midnight I let the children escape
longer than usual while I mused
over new and unproved forms of torture
that left no proof or mental stigma, and yet...
I stopped by the refrigerator.
The pack I'd been leisurely chasing
caught up with me from behind—I roared
and sent them off screaming and chortling.
The whimsical genius in me
who likes to gratify his little children's
love of persecution and the weird in general,
suddenly saw in a jar of mustard,
a new and diabolical way
to inflict distress on my young charges.
The urchins knew I'd stopped the chase—
they hid in the living room
and sent a small scout crawling on his belly
to test how volatile the kitchen might be.
I bayed like an entirely unstable lion,
sending the whole pack screaming
in circles of euphoria.
Unobserved, I opened the mustard,
scooped out just a touch, shut the jar,
quietly placed it back in the refrigerator,
turned out the lights one by one
til the entire house was worried and dark,
all the while snarling deep in my chest,
a dysfunctional and troubled werewolf.

The dark house wasn't a new ploy,
but effectively caused the little children
to run and moan with fear and joy.
Now silent, in a crouch, made my way
into the living room, behind the couch,
to wait for an experimental victim,
mustard on my fingertip,
listening to them whisper, planning nonsense.
Jaren, my nephew, careless and crazy,
stumbled against me in the dark and shrieked
"Uncle Jim's in the living room! Run!"
Because of the mustard
I didn't grab him as well as I might.
Jaren writhed, struggled and got away,
the whole group broke as one
and ran for their lives.
I loped after them,
knowing that one would fall
or be purposely tripped by his fellow pranksters;
and sure enough, Jaren fell and I was on him.
He screamed, "Noooooo!"
Upon occasion, the entire group would leap on me,
pummeling, barking, gnawing, pinching,
attempting to free their compatriot.
But on this night they chose to circle around us
to dance and mock. I held Jaren down,
my elbow against his chest, found his face
in the dark and stuck the dab of mustard
in his mouth just as someone flipped on a lamp.
Jaren's entire body and face went limp

surprised as anyone who'd ever lived,
he choked, gagged and screamed for real,
"AHHHHH! What is that!?"
He spit, writhed and fought
like a maniac in a comic book.
"It tastes like bug guts!"
Now that he'd been properly tormented,
I released him.
He jumped to his feet gagging
and giving witness, "Oh...My...God,"
sincerely seeking communion with the Almighty.
He started to retch again.
"I'm gonna throw up. What was that?"
"Torture," I said.
All five of the little desperadoes
looked at me with new respect and old fear.
Jaren started to cry, they all retreated
towards the TV room, keeping me in their sights.
I suppose they held a meeting,
while I sat on the couch and rested.
A few moments passed; they peeked around the corner
from the far end of the room,
all five including Jaren,
and appealed quietly, with new gravity,
"Torture us."

THE STATE'S POSITION
(Towards Me)

Philistine.
Oh, reprobate,
you deny me
your attention and courtesy.
I will lay
my laws on your
crooked brow
and troubled sneer.

Primitive,
you barbarian;
no sense
of what is mine.
You upset my constitution,
designed to protect
my land and heirs
from the likes of you.

Hooligan,
vulgar vandal,
can't you see
how beautiful
my money is;
how similarly sacred
church and state.
Are you blind?

TRAPPED
IN A FOOLISH INFINITY

My relationship with eternity is stuck—
feet and hands in concrete,
imagination suspended in time
tranquilized by music, books
and even poetry I suppose,
all keeping me here in the moment
instead of spread out all over
"Forever"
an idea told to me by a cabal
of women who believe
in Jesus and Buddha (even though
they didn't believe in each other),
in an age embroidered with
crystals and good intentions;
and I imagine if I could work
up a real and sincere meditation
(inevitably broken by thoughts
like these), something could be done,
infinity defined, now left behind—
but I can't so it's not and all that's
left is my sincere investigation
into the depths of the new age
of women, the portal of infinity

where I can get stuck
and unstuck never knowing
my place in Einstein's train,
yet appreciating
the lubricated trip, plugged into God,
Hallowed be thy name.

IN MIND
(Out of Sight)

There are trains
running out of my head
regularly
in every direction
all over the world
for thousands of miles
pulling strings
tight
nothing gets in
the trains go out
I taste the smoke
knowing it
wishing/

MY PRISON

It's midnight nearly all the time.
hours don't pass so much as deflate,
the air is numb, hearts beat
slower than a reptile,
no stars consent to be seen.

Birds dance with barbed wire,
mocking and mimicking captivity.
the clothes are frozen
like a drab and gaudy
mental institution.

There is food, so to speak,
chewed thoughtfully
in the Buddhist manner,
allowing sane humility
to crowd out the indigent rage.

Standing in the yard,
staring at the sky wondering
if it's the same rain
falling on hobos, real estate agents,
holding down the world.

The sky frames an imaginary moon,
lost in a court case
back in the world.
before the fall
from grace.

SHE RUNS...

lipstick smeared, wig in mouth
through the city
as far away as her muscular legs
hopelessly pumping, can carry her;
no thought offered to the horror
of another paper trail,
elevator ride over the sun
setting on the concrete city,
foolscap in her mouth
or paperclips up her ass;
fellow wage slaves left behind
mewling in stasis
begging their fax machines
to shut the fuck up;
        so...she runs,
shedding stockings, nails and shoes
steadily putting distance
between what's to come, what she wants,
whispering a blue incantation;
wishes she had some moisturizer,
the concrete as cruel to her feet
as the lunatic auditors
who mismanage the firm's affairs
while managing to sexually harass—
all to be implicated including
the Executive Officer who soared to the top
avoiding and delegating, portraying himself
as the son of Shakespeare and Machiavelli...

          leaving her the power behind the bone,
growing afraid of herself,
the night purple bruise
falling on the dinner crowds.

Crazed investors, senile retirees and stockholders
are met, and discover
she's on Valium, off the take,
on the run, down to her panties and bra
exciting packs of taxi cabs and worn commuters
wondering why the wig in her mouth...
          she runs...feet bleeding, eyes screaming,
accidentally inhaling a lock of auburn hair;
the endorphins raise a sense
of right and wrong,
the humiliation of a 50 year old
nearly naked bloodied woman on display—
fear makes her slowly trot in a half circle,
fix the wig firmly, and back
to the wrack and ruin of an empire
hoisted on her token sex
by dirty blind economic chance...

...she runs/

LIE
LIKE A NOVEL

Made the decision
to lie every
and all day,
like a novelist,
creating detail
from scratch and ink;
a book of lies
made from life,
even the pauses
will be false;
the truth won't allow
a hundred lovers
who need to be fed
silver dollars
and the unique,
washed down with lies
like chocolate water;
I can't sell
the difference,
the real is
a rich liar.